Dedication

*Dedicated to my parents who lit the lamp
and the children of the Maasai.*
Kioi Mbugua

To my daughter Murugi and other future leaders.
Kahare Miano

Inkishu
Myths and Legends of the Maasai

Acknowledgement

We gratefully acknowledge the assistance of OXFAM International for their assistance in providing transport and support for Kioi Mbugua on his travels into Maasailand to collect the data for these stories. We also thank Rev. Joseph L. Ole Kasio of Nairobi Translation Centre for his help with the Maasai language and translations.

Text by Kioi wa Mbugua
Edited by Bridget A. C. King
Poems by Goro wa Kamau
Photographs (c) Adrian Arbib
Cover sketch by Kahare Miano
Graphic Design by Katherine Mamai

Published by Jacaranda Designs, Ltd.
P.O. Box 76691 Nairobi, Kenya
Copyrights (c) Jacaranda Designs, Ltd.
First published 1994

ISBN 9966-884-97-1

Typeset in Palatino
Printed in Singapore by Singapore National Printers Ltd

Table of Contents

Foreword..(i)

Preface..(ii)

Inkishu: **Enkai's Great Gift**   Page 2
Original Art by Kang'ara wa Njambi

Enaiminie Enkiyio: **The Forest of the Lost Child**   Page 18
Original Art by Samwel Ngoje

    "Nasira"   Page 31
    Illustrated by Samwel Ngoje

    "Umbilical Cord"   Page 32
    Illustrated by Kang'ara wa Njambi

Oldoinyio Lenkai: **The Sacred Mountain**   Page 34
Original Art by Kahare Miano

    "Cattle Egret"   Page 52
    Illustrated by Kahare Miano

Ole Partukei: **The Warrior Who Turned Wild**   Page 54
Original Art by Godfrey Nyotumba

Foreword

Traditionally, Maasai children are taught community customs, social values and history through stories. Like the fairy tales in Europe, the characters of giants, greedy animals and fierce warriors in Maasai literature serve to warn, prepare and amuse children for their adult life to come.

Aptly titled, the book attaches particular importance to stories which tell of men and of '*Inkishu*', cattle. The Maasai are probably the most pastoral peoples of Africa and this book comments on the three essentials of their life: their God, their land and their cattle.

Four important Maasai tales are skilfully retold in this book. It is material which I shall use to teach my Kenya Broadcasting Corporation radio audience about the richness of Maasai customs and oral traditions. The stories are well written and presented from a recognisably Maasai perspective. The storylines have been maintained as closely as possible to the original Maasai language version. In their present form and style, they are now intelligible to the non-Maasai community and such a scholarly work should encourage more writers to collect and develop traditional stories to pass on to our children.

David K. Ole Tuukuo
Radio Producer
Kenya Broadcasting Corporation

Preface

The name Maasai is derived from the fact that they speak the Maa language. The Maasai people are Plains Nilotes, semi-nomadic pastoralists, who inhabit an area of just under 15,000 square miles in Kenya and 26,000 square miles in Tanzania, crossing between the two countries with total equanimity; in fact, they regard themselves as one community irrespective of such artificial boundaries. In the 19th century travellers told exaggerated tales of the bravery and courage of the Maasai people and this fierce reputation may well have saved the Maasai from Arab slave traders, who generally avoided them. Although they are herdsmen of domestic livestock, they co-exist with a remarkably rich variety of wildlife in a natural setting of splendid, but often parched, open spaces.

Traditionally, as soon as a Maasai boy was about seven years old he began going into the bush with his elder brothers and friends to learn how to look after the livestock. Girls stayed at home with their mothers and female relations helping to milk the cows, cook, draw water, fetch firewood or dung, sew skins and thread beads. By interacting with their elders, the children learned the family traditions as soon as they could understand them. Their grandmothers told them stories, riddles and proverbs which they in turn told to each other; stories such as these.

The stories in this anthology came about as a result of a journey I made with the OXFAM team who work with the Maasai people of the Narok district. I sat under the stars with Ole Parkisua, a wonderfully intelligent elder who, hunched over an open fire, would tell tales of Zamani, the times long passed. Well versed in traditional lore, Ole Parkisua had so much to impart to the next generation. Myths, genealogies, clan histories, songs and ceremonial rites were all stored up in his ancient skull, waiting to be handed on to perpetuate the consciousness of his people. Sadly, he knew that much of what he had learned and understood would soon vanish. Ole Parkisua is among the last survivors of a world which had no written records; a world in which traditions and histories were handed on orally; a world which may well end with his generation.

I felt it was time to tap the wisdom of the Maasai people and give it an infinite lifespan.

Kioi wa Mbugua
1994

Preamble

It is the convenient belief of the Maasai that, once upon a time, Enkai gave their ancestors all the cattle on earth. Hence, whenever and wherever they raided cattle it could not be said to be stealing, for were they not just taking back what was once their own?

The social and economic life of the Maasai centres around cattle. The different parts of the carcass can be used as food, medicine, utensils, clothing and adornment. Cattle signify wealth and confer status on their owner; they can be used instead of money, to legitimize marriages and as a symbol of religious significance. They are objects of affection and act as a bond in social relationships. To the Maasai, cattle give meaning to life, in fact they mean life itself. The Maasai are *'Iltung'ana loo Nkishu'* or 'People of Cattle'.

Inkishu:
Enkai's Great Gift

In the distant past, according to oral tradition, all the cattle in the world belonged to the Maasai. This ancient legend tells how cattle were first given to the Maasai people.

The ancient settlement of Kerio in the northern Rift Valley of Kenya was surrounded by great hills. Here lived Maasinta, the father of the Maasai. He and his family lived among the vast herds of wild animals which roamed the open plains and valleys, but at certain times of the year, when the animals migrated to search for fresh pastures, the family always went hungry.

At such times, the old man and his servant Oltorroboni spent all their time hunting for meat to feed the family. Eventually Maasinta felt too old and tired to hunt any longer. After much thought, Maasinta prayed to Enkai to give him animals which would not disappear into the wilderness but belong to him and his family for all time.

"Stand at the edge of the great valley on the twilight of the tenth day," Enkai instructed Maasinta, "for then you will receive my answer."

On the appointed day, Maasinta sacrificed a fine wild buffalo in honour of Enkai. The father of the Maasai did not eat a single morsel of the precious meat but threw the whole carcass onto a big fire. As the meat roasted, the smoke of the fire drifted up into the sky above the hills. Maasinta was engrossed in deep prayers when from the hills came a deep, rolling rumble of thunder that filled his ears. Overwhelmed, he again heard the voice of Enkai:

"Build a large *enkang*. Let it be a homestead where you and the animals may live together."

With the help of his family, Maasinta erected many small, dome-shaped huts out of strong sticks and bark fibre. They covered the huts with a layer of thick mud to keep out the heat of the sun and the dry swirling dust. When the *enkang* was completed, Enkai looked down and saw that it was well constructed. He then told Maasinta to cut down some thorn bushes and form them into a large circle in the middle of the *enkang*.

4

5

6

When this too was done, Enkai spoke once more:

"When the new moon appears in the sky, you will receive my gift of animals. You, Maasinta, have always been respectful and obedient of my wishes. Now, to receive the gift which I shall send you, there is one thing you must remember: No one must utter a single sound until the last creature has descended from heaven."

Maasinta did not consider it important to tell Oltorroboni the details of Enkai's plan. When the moon appeared, Maasinta went to the edge of the valley where he eagerly awaited his gift from heaven. While praying, he heard the familiar sound of rolling thunder and Enkai's voice came out of the clouds:

"I have chosen you and your descendants to be the guardians of my special creation. This creation will keep you and your people well supplied with nourishing milk and meat; it will guard you from hunger and thirst; it will provide clothes for your bodies and shelter for your families. These precious animals shall be called '*Inkishu*'.

After waiting patiently, Maasinta heard a mighty roaring like a crash of thunder, but remembering Enkai's words he was neither surprised nor astonished. There was a flash of lightning as the sky grew darker. Out of the leaden skies came a long, broad leather thong. Down the thong came hundreds of animals which began to fill the

huge thorny enclosure, crowding one against the other. They were huge beasts with horns on their heads and hooves on their feet. The coats of the fine bulls glistened with health, the females were blessed with deep udders and the sturdy calves bleated and mooed loudly. Thus, due to Maasinta's faith and Enkai's love of mankind, Maasinta's prayer was answered.

The thorny enclosure was crowded with the animals and Oltorroboni grew so excited and astonished that he exclaimed:

"*Ayie yie.. Nkumok oleng* - There are so many!"

As he uttered the last word a flash of lightning burned the thong, severing the link with Enkai. Neither on that day nor on any other were more *inkishu* sent from heaven.

8

9

Furious, Maasinta cursed Oltorroboni. "Through your foolish outburst you have broken my promise to Enkai. Go away from here and never return. Live in the forest and may the wild animals be your *inkishu*, for you will have none of mine. May the milk of my *inkishu* be poison to you for ever more."

Maasinta's family were filled with excitement as they dodged the hooves of the animals in the enclosure. The eyes of the men glistened with pride and the women saw that the beasts were fine and healthy.

"Truly these cattle are a great gift. No other people have ever received a gift of such value. Now we know that Enkai really loves the Maasai," they said.

Maasinta gave all the red cattle to his first wife and all the black cattle to his second wife. The descendants of the first wife were known as '*Odomong'i*', the people of the red cattle, and those of the second

11

wife as 'Orok-Kiteng', people of the black cattle. All the Maasai, up to this very day, can trace their descent to these two wives.

Meanwhile, the banished Oltorroboni pleaded with Enkai to give him cattle of his own, but in vain. Instead he was given the animals of the forest and the plains. Oltorroboni was unhappy and went back once more to Enkai to plead for cattle but again he was refused. Instead Enkai gave Oltorroboni a bow and arrow saying: "Use these to kill the animals you need to survive."

For four days Oltorroboni went without food. It had rained and the bowstring had snapped. Oltorroboni was hungry, yet there was so much food available. Once more he went back to plead with Enkai:

"Enkai, do you still refuse to give me cattle?" he pleaded.

"I do," answered the great deity, "for I have given you the animals of the plains and forest to provide your needs. You must learn to use what I have given you."

14

Oltorroboni went to live in the forest. There he found a snake and an elephant.

One day he said to the snake: "My friend, why does my body itch so that I have to scratch whenever you breathe on me?".

The snake replied: "Oh, my father, I do not know. I do not intend to harm you."

Oltorroboni remained silent, but the same evening he picked up his club and struck the snake on the head, killing it instantly.

The following day the elephant asked Oltorroboni: "Where is our friend the snake?"

Oltorroboni replied that he did not know, but the elephant, being wise and all-knowing, knew that the man had killed it.

A drought fell over the land and Oltorroboni could no longer draw water in the river. Instead he drew water from deep pools. After a time all the pools, except for one, became dry. The elephant and her calf used to go to this water hole and eat the green grass which grew around it. When they had had enough to eat, they would drink at the pool. Lying down in the pool to cool their bodies, they stirred up the mud so that when Oltorroboni came to drink, he could not draw clean water. In anger, Oltorroboni made an arrow and shot the mother elephant, killing her with one blow.

"Oltorroboni is bad," the baby elephant said, "I will not live with him any longer. First of all he killed the snake and now he has killed my mother."

The young elephant was angry and moved away to live in another part of the country where there was fresh grass to eat and plenty of water to drink. When Maasinta heard this sad story he told the elephant:

"Do not fear Oltorroboni for I will protect you from his arrow whenever he dares to attack you."

Maasinta and his family established a friendly relationship with the wild animals, learning to live amongst them in peace and never killing them for food, except in times of great hardship. They tended well the cattle which Enkai had given them; their numbers multiplied and the people prospered.

But Oltorroboni has been hunting for food with his bow and arrow ever since.

From that mythical hour, the whole culture of the Maasai people has developed through their contact with cattle. Every part of the cow is used for some purpose or another. The relationship between a Maasai and his cattle is a sacred one, for neither could exist without the other in the dry, parched grasslands of East Africa.

Preamble

This forest, also known as the Loita Forest, still exists and can be found in the Loita area of the Narok District of Kenya. It remains an area of undisturbed nature in the wide lands of the Maasai and is much valued for the many benefits it bestows: water, wild fruits and berries, honey and lush grass can be found there at even the driest times of the year. In addition, many of the trees have valuable medicinal properties which can be exploited. Maasai children love to eat the wild fruits and berries. One of these looks like a kidney so they give it the Maasai name 'Nkayaku'j', kidney. They also enjoy the fruit of the rain tree, 'Olng'aboli, and that of a plains plant with a flower like a petunia which is called 'Ol-oiropiji'. When they should be looking after the calves, many children neglect their duties in favour of searching for the special fruit, so there is even a Maasai rhyme about this:

"Children, where are the calves?"   "They have strayed."
"What is that you are eating?"   "Ol-oiropiji roots!"

Grass holds a prominent place in many Maasai stories as it is the primary source of food for their beloved cattle. The Maasai hold grass blades to symbolise peace and when moving from one village to another they tie grass onto their gourds as a link between one place and another. If a traveller sees a fallen tree on the road, he pulls up some grass and throws it onto the tree to ward off evil or misfortune.

Enaiminie Enkiyio:
The Forest Of The Lost Child

Long before your grandparents were born, there lived a lively young daughter of the Maasai whose name was Nasira. Every evening she would sit with her grandmother around the fireside listening to the age old stories which had been handed down in just such a manner for many generations.

Many of the stories Nasira was told recalled the creation of the Maasai people, how the Maasai got their cattle from Enkai, the cunning nature of the wild animals, the brave deeds of men and the wicked deeds of ogres. At the end of each story the little girl would ask many questions which her grandmother would be glad to answer.

The stories that Nasira liked the best were those about the forest. This huge forest lay at the edge of the Maasai lands and many tales were told about its mysteries. Once, Nasira's grandmother told her this story:

"A group of Maasai morans made a camp in the middle of the mysterious forest. On their way back from a cattle raid, some of the morans got lost in the dense forest. The lost morans beat the trees with their clubs to make an echo so that their colleagues could find them. When, however, the search party reached the spot from which the noise came, there was no sign of the lost morans. They had totally vanished! Since that time, those poor morans were never seen again."

Nasira grew to be a hard working and respectful child. She fetched water and firewood, tended the calves and helped with the milking. Although she would do her chores diligently, she was always attracted to the mysterious forest. During the dry season, when the cattle were taken into the forest to graze, she would plead to go with them. Often she would volunteer to pick the berries which the family loved from the edge of the forest. Grandmother always warned Nasira not to wander too deeply into the forest in search of the berries and the little girl obeyed her, anxious not to get lost like the morans of long ago.

Then came a time of severe drought. The land lost its cloak of green and gold and became dusty and brown. The animals ate the grass on the plains until nothing remained. The water in the streams near the homestead dried up and it was a time of hunger and thirst for both man and beast. Driven by a strong desire to find juicy berries, the little girl wandered deep into the forest. She found an abundance of luscious berries where no one had ventured before and filled her beaded leather bag to the brim before turning to go back home.

As she walked, she learned more of the secrets of the ancient forest. The thick undergrowth hid many animals. Startled impala and shy duikers leapt out of her way in surprise. Even a short-sighted buffalo trotted past her, crashing its way through the bush and sending up clouds of butterflies and insects in its wake.

20

Reaching a clear flowing stream at the foot of a small hill, Nasira clambered down to the water's edge and rested for a while. After eating a few of the berries she continued on her way and was coming closer to the edge of the forest when she met a group of older girls. She recognised them as coming from her own village.

"Where have you sprung from?" they asked rudely. "You're a long way from home. What do you have in that bag? Show us what you're hiding."

"I've come from deep within the forest," Nasira replied politely. "My family is hungry and I've been picking berries for them."

The older girls were hungry too. They snatched the leather bag from Nasira's hands and ran away with it, helping themselves to the contents until all the berries were gone. The little girl sank onto the leafy ground and sobbed bitterly. Now she was empty handed and she had promised her family that she would find some food.

"I can't go home with an empty bag," she sighed sadly. "It's late and I'm so tired but I must go back and find some more berries." She vowed this time to show her precious finds to neither friends nor strangers .

Picking up the empty bag, which the older girls had abandoned, she walked once more into the forest. Wearily she stumbled on in search of a new source of berries. As Nasira walked deeper and deeper into the forest the berries became bigger and better. Again, she filled her bag to the brim. Having gathered enough at last, she turned to go back home. Unfortunately, she had wandered further than ever before and was not sure which way to go.

The light was fading and strange noises frightened little Nasira as she sought desperately for a way out of the forest. In her panic she ran this way and that, searching for a path which she recognised. Thoughts raced round her mind. She remembered her grandmother's story of the lost *morans* who had vanished in this very forest. Like them, she attempted to draw attention to her plight by feebly beating a tree trunk with a broken branch, but her efforts were in vain. She fell to the ground in despair as darkness consumed the forest.

Back home, the family of the little girl became alarmed when she did not return that evening. The family looked for her in neighbouring villages and in the bush surrounding the forest. Two days passed and still she did not come home. Nobody had seen her since the day she first went into the forest. The girls who had snatched her bag were too ashamed and scared to tell anyone that they had seen Nasira going back into the forest. They feared that they would be accused of killing the little girl.

Kones, a respected elder, sent word for the *morans* to help. Coming from a distant *manyatta*, they appeared carrying their spears and shields.

"One of our daughters is missing," Kones told them. "We fear that the forest has swallowed her up. Go! Search the forest diligently and bring Nasira safely home to us."

Kones gave the warriors his blessing by pouring honey-wine and milk onto the ground. The women in turn sprinkled the warrior *morans* with milk from a special gourd as they sent them on their way. The *morans* set off bravely to scour the dense forest for the missing child.

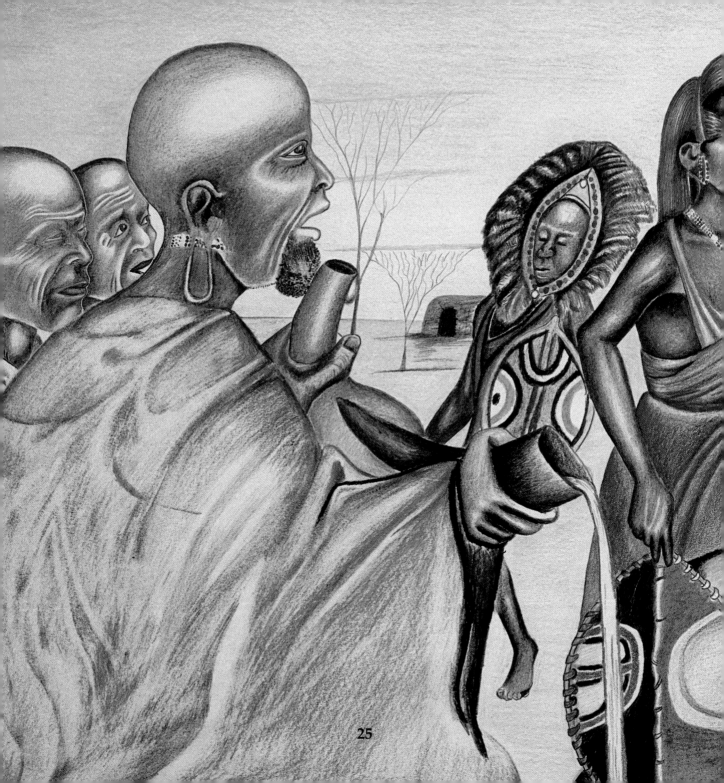

After two days the little girl's family went to the *manyatta* of the *morans* to await their return. The women took gourds of milk and tied grass onto their skirts to ward off bad omens. As they faced the morning star, they prayed:

"Enkai to whom we pray,
Return our child to us,
Remember us Enkai,
Let our child live,
Bless all the Maasai."

On the fourth day the warriors were sighted. The women alerted the waiting group with their traditional ululation. As the warriors came closer, the women searched amongst them for some evidence of the little girl. When they saw no sign of the lost child, their ululation turned to wild sobs of grief. Now they knew for certain that the little girl must be gripped fast in the cruel claws of the mysterious forest.

When Kones the elder heard the news he grieved deeply. The *manyatta* was silent as the people bowed their heads in sorrow. The younger children sobbed and the grandmother cried aloud in grief for her lost grandaughter. As they sat around the evening fire, the women missed the warm company of the lively little girl.

Since that sad time, the Maasai have named the forest *"Enaiminie Enkiyio"*, or The Forest of the Lost Child. The Forest of the Lost Child is still an undisturbed wilderness in the wide lands of the Maasai and remains surrounded by a lasting aura of mystery.

29

30

Nasira

Nasira,
Daughter of Maa
I salute you my love!

How beautiful you look in your coils of brass
I see the sun playing on your colourful beads of glass
Will you give me your rainbow coloured belt, Nasira
So that it may adorn my shield?

Nasira,
How I adore those earrings,
Hanging so from your earlobes
I can hear them sing as you walk.

My wife,
I hear you pray
That God may light the moon
in your life
And grant you children
as plentiful as the stars
In the dark sky.

Then shall I slaughter for you
the fattest of my rams.
The sweet smell of child's urine
shall fill the house
And you shall be shaven with milk.

Oh, Nasira,
Daughter of Maa,
You of the great house of Laibon,
I hail you my beloved.

Umbilical Cord

Heaven give us cattle
And rain
Send the rain in torrents
Then the grass will grow
In plenty
The cattle shall eat
In mouthfuls
And the people will become healthy
On meat.
Oh heaven,
Send us cattle
And rain.

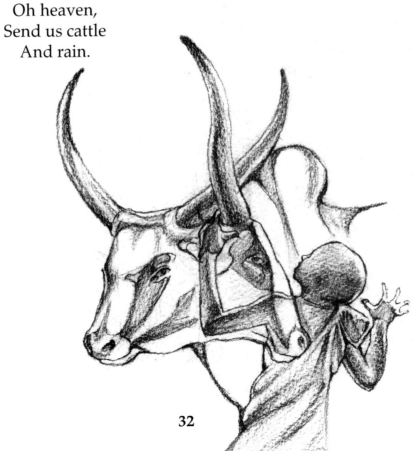

Preamble

In Africa outstanding mountains and hills are generally regarded as sacred and given religious significance. Oldoinyio Lenkai, a sacred mountain of the Maasai, is found in Tanzania, not far from the Kenyan border. The Maasai hold Mount Lenkai dearly for their concept of God is associated with anything that is highly revered. The Bavenda and Shona of Zimbabwe consider the Matopos mountains to be the place of God's manifestations, while the Lang'i of Uganda connect God with all hills and therefore places to be avoided, although Mount Agoro is used for pilgrimage. These mountains and hills are in no way thought to be God; they simply give a concrete manifestation of His being and His presence. (J.S. Mbiti, African Religions and Philosophy)

The Maasai word 'Enkai', God, is also used for thunderstorms and volcanoes. Sacrifice is part of their religious belief and for this they use the sacred cattle.

Oldoinyio Lenkai:
The Sacred Mountain

Ole Parkisua is an elder of the Illoita group of the Maasai peoples of Kenya. This story was told to him by his grandmother, a long time ago, when he was just a child. As the old man retells the tale, he recalls with nostalgia the power of the great god of the mountain in the history of the Maasai people.

In the vast sprawling land of the Maasai is a pillar of rock called *Oldoinyio Lenkai*, the Mountain of God. An active volcano, this mountain has always played an important role in the life of the Maasai. Its moods are thought to express pleasure or anger with the people who live within her shadow. An almost spiritual relationship has evolved with this fiery deity which from time to time throws sheets of flame and moulten lava into the skies.

The Maasai also call their sacred mountain "*Oldoinyio Osira Lenkai*" meaning 'The Striped Mountain of God', referring to the streams of ashes which often pour down from the crater. When the mountain is in a good mood, the spirits and hopes of the Maasai people are high.

The god of Mount Lenkai is consulted when calamities befall the people; disasters such as long spells of drought, epidemics, starvation, barrenness in women and bewitchment by enemies are taken to Enkai', the God of the Mountain, to give his judgement. Within Mount Lenkai lives a spirit called *Kirim* who acts as a messenger between Enkai and his people.

In the distant days of memory, the Maasai faced a severe drought. Many of their precious cattle died from hunger and thirst and the drought was so widespread that no new pastures could be found. To compound this tragedy, a terrible new disease broke out which affected man and beast alike, leaving many in the belly of the hyena. Half the people and their livestock lay dead or dying and those who remained were in danger of following them.

After long and worried discussions, the Maasai elders decided that they must visit Mount Lenkai to find the cause of the disasters that threatened their very existence. Looking among the few leaders that remained, the elders chose Ole Sankale to represent his people before the great deity

Ole Sankale came from a fine family which had produced many diviners in the past. He accepted the task with pride but as he thought more about what he must do, he grew afraid of his mission. If he were to fail, the whole future of the Maasai people could be jeopardised. However, he organised a group of elders and *morans* to accompany him.

Emin siriri kina.
The clever child hears the secrets

"*Lo Moruak!* You Chosen Ones! Listen carefully to what I have to say," he commanded, striking the ground with a club of rhinoceros horn for emphasis. "Tomorrow, before the skies grow light, we will leave our home in silence. It will take many days for us to reach the Mountain of God, and each man will behave with dignity in the manner befitting a noble Maasai. Carry with you a knobbed stick and a fly whisk and take enough milk to enable you to face the long journey. The strongest donkeys will be chosen to carry your gourds of milk and your cowhides for sleeping. We will drive before us a black ox to be our sacrifice to the God of the Mountain."

The procession left before dawn the next day. The women, dressed in their finest beaded necklaces, bracelets and earrings, lined the well trodden path shouting words of encouragement as their menfolk passed by:

> "*Go far and wide and may Enkai be with you!*"
> "*Go south and bring back Enkai's treasures in your hands!*"
> "*May you have success even though the path is dry!*"

39

The chosen group walked across the plains, ridges and valleys, through dense bush and thickly forested ravines, each day drawing closer to the great mountain. As they travelled across the dry country, the weariness and hunger of the Maasai increased, for it is not in their culture to eat the meat of wild beasts. The antelope were also on the move in search of better grazing, for the drought had reached far and wide and all were suffering. Wildebeest, rhino, zebra and lion watched the Maasai pass by, but so fierce and purposeful were they, that the animals were intimidated and kept out of the way.

As darkness engulfed the sky at the end of each burning day, Ole Sankale and his companions sought refuge in a friendly *enkang* or homestead. Wearily wrapping themselves in skins, they fell into an exhausted sleep.

41

When the group reached the foot of *Oldoinyio Osira Lenkai*, Ole Sankale led them to the holy ground *'Orkuroto'*. Many Maasai had gathered together here to consult the great God of the Mountain and find solutions to their various troubles.

As tradition demanded, Ole Sankale and his followers carried horns full of oil as a sacrifice to Enkai. When *Kirim* appeared, the Sonjo mediator received the horns one after the other and the ceremonies began.

At last it was the turn of Ole Sankale. He took a purple cloth called an *'Enanka'* from beneath his robe and tied the cloth around his head as a symbol of the royal Maasai and to show his respect for the great God of the Mountain. Speaking through the Sonjo mediator, Ole Sankale besought:

> *"O Holy One. We are greatly troubled.*
> *For many moons now we have had no rain.*
> *The grass is finished, the rivers and streams are dry.*
> *The cattle, our special gift from Enkai, are dying daily.*
> *Our wives and children suffer from lack of milk and meat.*
> *Even our brave morans are weak and weary from hunger and thirst.*
> *Save us, O Great One. Tell us what we must do to appease you.*
> *Restore our lands to rich and green pastures."*

A deep voice came from the midst of the mountain, accompanied by a thunderous sound that rumbled through the clouds, saying:

"I see your troubles. Their cause is plain."

"For many moons you have been at war with the clans of your area. So much death and destruction has greatly displeased me. The death and destruction you now suffer is a result of your own actions."

"Return now to your lands. Seek unity and peace with your neighbours."

"When this is done, the demons will be cast out, the sick will be healed. Rain will once more fall over your pastures."

Ole Sankale bowed his head in understanding. It was true. For many months the clans had been warring among themselves and many people had suffered. While battles had been waged, the herds had been neglected and forced to graze in one area. That area had suffered severe erosion from over grazing and the problem had grown worse.

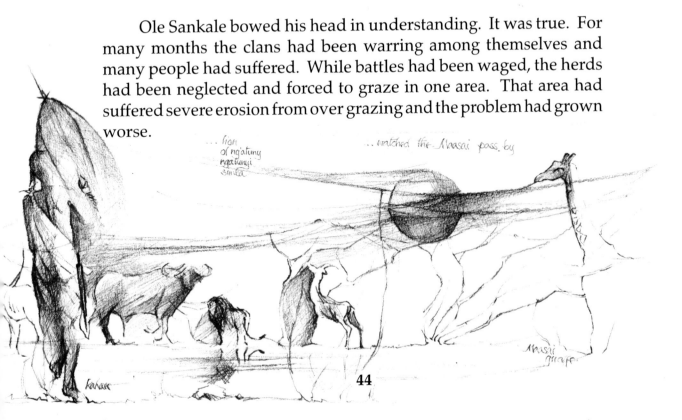

Lifting his rhinoceros horn club above his head, Ole Sankale faced the mountain and gave thanks for the blessings he had received. He implored once again that rain might fall on his parched homeland:

"I pray my Enkai,
My Enkai who is in Heaven.
Enkai guard our children and cattle.
Enkai give us health.
Let us be at peace.
Let the souls of our people be refreshed,
Remember us, O Enkai."

The black ox was sacrificed and its roasted meat shared out among those gathered on the holy ground. When the ceremonies were over, the remaining bones and vegetation were thrown into a huge fire and the ashes buried as Maasai tradition demanded. Gathering up his possessions, Ole Sankale led his followers away from the sacred ground and began their long homeward trek.

As they journeyed, the mighty peaks of the mountain disappeared into the distance behind them and the rocky hills and trees of their own country came into sight. The sight of herds of cattle and the sound of their distant bells encouraged the weary travellers to move on before hunger and exhaustion overtook them. Early on the fifth morning, Ole Sankale and his group arrived at their own *enkang*.

Many elders, warriors, women and children were there to welcome home the weary travellers. The women gave them gourds full of milk to show love and thankfulness for their safe return. A fine ox was slaughtered and the women, decked with the leaves of the holy *Oreteti* or fig tree, sang and danced in praise of Ole Sankale and his group. They sprinkled the elders with sweet honey and milk. A new fire was kindled in the middle of the cattle enclosure to signify the end of an era and the beginning of a new life.

49

50

That night, Ole Sankale sat down with the elders of the clan and told them of the warning and the promise that the God of the Mountain had given. The elders seated around Ole Sankale nodded and spat into the ground to show their respect for his words. They agreed to live peacefully with the other clans and immediately to cease their warring ways. Soon, as predicted, rain fell once more on the parched lands and life returned to normal.

To this day, the Maasai from as far as Mao-narok, Laikipia, Loliondo and Ngorongoro districts walk to Mount Lenkai to appease the great deity and receive his blessings and protection from misfortune.

"Our forefathers spoke to the God of the Mountain and so will the children of the Maasai."

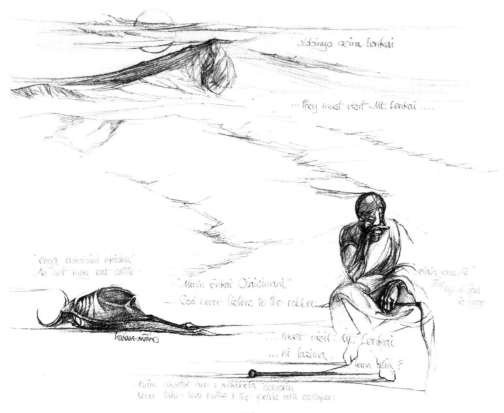

The Cattle Egret

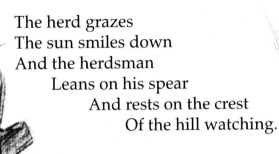

The herd grazes
The sun smiles down
And the herdsman
    Leans on his spear
        And rests on the crest
           Of the hill watching.

The cattle egret
Pure white
Like milk in the gourd
Perches on the anthill hump
Of the lead bull
And pecks,
Removing the ticks
From his back.

The herdsman watches
A cool breeze blows down
From the distant mountains
Over the plains
His voice carries across the grasslands
Gently, like an egret in flight
The herdsman sings the praises
Of his prize bull.

Preamble

The moran or warriors, form a very important social unit among the Maasai. After circumcision they live in a separate enclosure called an emanyatta where their mothers and elder sisters have built houses for them. The houses are built in circles, with the doors facing into the centre and the livestock are herded into the centre of the circle at night for protection. The moran are not allowed to eat alone, cannot drink milk from their own family's herds, and always go around in groups.

In this special camp, the warriors receive instruction and guidance from specially selected elders known as Olpiron. The youths form strong fellowships known as 'age groups' which emphasize sharing and communal ownership. The supreme values of these age groups are egalitarian solidarity and generosity. The members of an age group regard each other as lifelong brothers.

In former times, each warrior tried to kill at least one lion in single combat in order that he might be allowed to wear the lion's mane on his head. The moran do not cut their hair, for this would make them lose their strength and courage. When it reaches the length of about one foot, the hair is dressed with fat and is then twisted into long spirals resembling string. These spirals are held together with strips of raw hide so that they form pigtails. After a certain time, the morans' heads are shaved by their mothers in a ceremony which marks a change in their status to that of junior elders. Only after this has taken place are Maasai men permitted to take a wife.

Ole Partukei:
The Warrior Who Turned Wild

Once, on the open plains of Kenya, there lived a great Maasai warrior known as Ole Partukei, a mighty giant of a man with extraordinary physical strength and matted shoulder-length hair. He had amazing eyesight and his wild, protruding eyes could spot prey from far away. This great warrior roamed the vast plains and forests of Maasailand without the slightest fear. He was so strong that if he caught a buffalo by the horns, fight and struggle as it might, it could not get away from his grasp. Lions cringed and made way for Ole Partukei as he walked arrogantly amongst them, while terrified leopards crouched, snarling, out of sight.

The *morans*, the famed warriors of the Maasai, must single handedly hunt and kill a lion to show their bravery. This is always a difficult and dangerous task, armed only with a spear and a shield. However, when Ole Partukei hunted for lions the other *morans* could only stand by and watch in awe as he killed the fiercest beast with one powerful thrust of his spear.

As a hero among the fierce Maasai, Ole Partukei was awarded many tokens in recognition of his achievements as an outstanding warrior. Headdresses made from lions' manes, special bracelets and earrings and other ornaments were heaped upon him, while his shield bore the much coveted white star of bravery, showing that he never retreated in battle.

When the mighty Ole Partukei went to *olpul*, he used to devour a whole bull all by himself while his companions went hungry. The famished warriors dared not complain about Ole Partukei's greed in case they too became a target for his violent anger.

As time went by, Ole Partukei's voracious appetite could not be satisfied within the *manyatta*, so with his servant Murunya Nkiyiaa, he decided to leave. The giant and his servant went to live in the forest where an abundant supply of wild animals provided him with plenty of meat. He grew ever fatter. Occasionally, when the wild warrior brought back a carcass, Murunya would sing a cynical song of praise as he tended the fire and roasted the meat:

> *"Ole Partukei, Oitalala endaata*
> *Otanapa nolaiki Meturua enapita*
> *Enjipati Olalae ntare tikitam*
> *Empukoro nairish Olkiteng le ntawuo*
> *Tenelo Merrorro tialo enaraa*
> *Netukuny te nkutuk entanu natong'ua*
> *Nemeisho enkitome naitaa ngotonye"*

> Ole Partukei, who hunts far and wide,
> Can devour incredible loads of meat;
> Twenty sheep to him is just a taste,
> Eating a young ox is almost starvation.
> He is surrounded by rotten, stinking meat
> Which he cannot even share with his poor mother
> Because of his insatiable greed.

Turning to a wild life in the bush, Ole Partukei acquired many animal traits. Uncovered, except for his own thickly matted body hair, he uttered animal-like grunts and growls that sounded quite inhuman. He always slept either out in the open or under thorny bushes. The animals grew to know and fear him, keeping well away from his lair.

Whenever Ole Partukei had exhausted the supply of wild game in an area he moved on to establish a new base camp in the forest, becoming a source of fear and misery to the people living nearby. He constantly raided their cattle and other livestock and none dared to

stop him. Even the fiercest of warriors refused to track down the mighty giant for fear of his incredible strength and ferocious anger. Occasionally a villager would catch a glimpse of Ole Partukei. Safely back home in his village, the trembling man would tell fearsome tales of his encounter with the wild giant. Many found it hard to believe that the now wild man used to be one of their own people.

"*Oosho!*", exclaimed a Maasai elder when he heard of his insatiable appetite, "*Meuputayu emala naudo kurum*", "this man is like a leaking gourd that cannot be filled".

One day, Ole Partukei went on a raid with his servant, Murunya. Reaching a pasture not far away where a herd of healthy cattle were grazing, they spotted an extremely fat ox. The *moran* guarding the herd had kept his sword sharp just in case the hungry giant came to steal his cattle. Seeing the great man approach, the *moran* hid behind a bush, too frightened to confront Ole Partukei, but not wanting to desert his post entirely. He watched as the wild man siezed the fat ox by the tail and began to drag it away. Outraged at such blatant theft, the *moran* threw his sword at Ole Partukei, striking him in the shoulder. In terror at his own daring, the *moran* ran away before the wild man could see him and give chase. Ole Partukei felt the slight prick of the sword as it entered his flesh and thought that Murunya was tapping him on the shoulder.

"What's wrong?" bellowed Ole Partukei.

"Nothing, sir," replied Murunya surprised for he had not seen the *moran's* attack. Before he could say more, the wild man had broken the neck of the ox with a single blow and dragged it off towards the forest.

Without feeling the slightest pain from the sword still stuck in his body, Ole Partukei strode through the forest leaving his servant far behind.

Later, when Murunya arrived panting at the meat camp, Ole Partukei said:

"There's sweat dripping down my back. Wipe it off."

"*Ai, aii,...* master" Murunya gasped in horror, "that's not sweat, it's blood. There's a sword stuck in your shoulder!"

Ole Partukei pulled out the sword as if it were a splinter and threw it away, not aware how badly he was injured.

"Who did this?" he roared.

"I don't know," whimpered Murunya. "It must have been one of the *morans* who were guarding the herd."

As angry as a wounded lion, Ole Partukei strode off back to the plains to find his attacker and take his revenge. By this time, the remaining cattle had been driven back to the *enkang*, the homestead of the owner. Ole Partukei followed the cattle tracks to the homestead and, from behind a fence, he overheard his attacker boasting to his fellow warriors:

"I taught the wild man a lesson he will not forget. He will not survive the deep wound I gave him with my sword," crowed the *moran* warming his hands at the fire.

His friends were horrified. "What have you done? You'll get us all into trouble now."

Ole Partukei's sudden and ferocious attack took them completely by surprise. In panic, the startled *morans* started to run away, but he was too fast for them. Catching the boasting *moran* by the leg he hurled him head first into a thorny bush. Then he tore up a tree trunk by its roots and raced after the fleeing *morans*, wielding it like a club. He caught one after another, knocking them all down until the homestead was littered with wounded *morans*. Having taken his revenge, the wild man returned satisfied to his camp.

61

Time passed and a severe drought spread across the land; the short grass turned brown and the rivers dried up. Many times the moon waxed and waned without bringing a change in the weather. The Maasai and their cattle were dying and most families made the desperate decision to move away from their traditional lands in search of new pastures for their livestock.

Only one man, Lankas, decided to remain in the land of his fathers. The forest was now the only place in the vicinity where green grass could be found, but this forest was the home of the dreaded Ole Partukei. Lankas had been a close friend of Ole Partukei when they were *morans* and because of this friendship, he hoped to persuade his old friend to let him graze his animals in the forest. Nervously he went to speak to the fearsome wild man.

"Ole Partukei, my old friend. I throw myself on your mercy at this time of great trouble. You are the acknowledged master of this forest and it is known that no one may graze their cattle here without your permission. However, in the name of our old friendship, I beg you, let me bring my animals into your forest to find food before they die."

"Lankas, my old friend" replied Ole Partukei his eyes gleaming with greed. "Bring hither your cattle, sheep and goats. Feel free to roam safely in my territory. I will gladly share this vast forest with you."

Much relieved and delighted, Lankas herded his cattle, sheep and goats into the forest to graze. As Maasai custom demanded, he presented Ole Partukei with a fine bull to seal the agreement they had made.

All went well until one sorrowful, shameful day when Ole Partukei was wandering through the forest and caught sight of his friend's impressive herd of cattle.

"*Woyie, woyie*! What a lot of fat bulls my old friend Lankas keeps on my land! Why should he have so many while I have none? I generously share my forest with him, therefore he should share his cattle with me," he reasoned.

So, overcome by his insatiable greed, Ole Partukei decided to raid his friend's herd. Once having made this treacherous decision he siezed the opportunity straight away, knowing that Lankas was visiting another region. Choosing the most beautiful ox with a red head and red spots on its back, he dragged it back to his camp and immediately ate it all. As soon as he had finished that one he went back for another and yet another. When Lankas finally returned from his safari, he was furious that the agreement they had made had been broken in his absence.

"My bulls! My bulls! Where are my precious bulls?" he cried. "I gave Ole Partukei my best bull and now he has stolen three more of my finest animals. He has treated his oldest friend like an enemy. "*Kurro milau eninang*", 'trouble comes to those who look for it'. I curse him by the blood of the fine bull that sealed our agreement, and swear that I will have my revenge."

Burning with hatred and the desire to avenge himself, Lankas visited a hunting friend to acquire some poisoned arrows. When the hunter heard that the arrows were to kill Ole Partukei he was delighted, for Ole Partukei had made hunting very difficult in the forest. Pleased that Lankas would attack his enemy, he gave him the most lethal poison that could be found in the forest. Tracking down Ole Partukei, Lankas found him at his campsite, feasting on a freshly killed hippo. Hiding behind a bush a good distance away from his foe, Lankas took his time to aim carefully before releasing three of the poisoned arrows. The first arrow flew above the giant's head, the second grazed his shoulder, but the third struck deeply into the flesh of his huge arm.

"Wou! Wou!..." roared Ole Partukei in rage looking round for his attacker, but Lankas was not to be seen. He had seen the arrow strike the mighty giant and had fled deep into the forest.

Ole Partukei wrenched the arrow out of his arm and saw the remains of the thick black poison on the arrowhead. Realising that he must act quickly to stop the poison from spreading, he wrapped a leather thong around his arm, then sucked at the poison and spat it out. He bellowed to Murunya.

"Make me a healing draught from the bladder of a heifer, my herbal potions and a lump of fat. Quickly man, before the poison takes effect."

When this potion was prepared he gulped it down without delay. Before long he felt the pain go away and his strength returned to normal.

The next day, Lankas crept cautiously back to the campsite to find out whether his foe was dead or alive. Seeing Ole Partukei eating heartily and obviously in good health, Lankas carefully prepared his bow and remaining arrows for another attack. This time he moved closer and scored a precise blow on the ankle joint that sent the great warrior writhing and screaming in agony. The small metal point of the hunter's arrow lodged deeply in the bone. Ole Partukei tried to pull out the arrow but the arrowhead remained firmly embedded. As the poison entered his body, Ole Partukei slumped to the ground and growled in mortal agony. From a safe distance Lankas watched his mighty enemy fall. Knowing this time the wound was fatal, Lankas hurried out of the forest.

Murunya prepared the foul medicine once again in an attempt to save his wounded master. Ole Partukei drank the potion, but this time in vain. As the pain grew harsher and his strength drained away, he recognised that this was indeed a mortal blow. Ole Partukei lost all hope of recovery, but facing death like the great warrior he had once been, he called on Murunya to listen to his last wishes:

"Bring me my spear, my shield, my headdress and my lion skin. Dress me up like the brave warrior I was in my youth."

Murunya wept great tears of sorrow as he adorned his master's body for the last time. With care he decorated the massive body of his master with the special necklaces, bracelets and beads, the lion skins and the headdress that only the bravest and most honoured of warriors was allowed to wear. The shield with the white star of honour was placed on his arm, and a long spear with a freshly honed killing edge was strapped to his fist. When Murunya had finished, Ole Partukei looked like the bravest *moran* ever to face a great battle.

Using every ounce of his strength, Murunya hauled his dying master to his feet and supported him against the trunk of the mighty *Oreteti* tree. On his feet and facing the setting sun in full battle regalia, the spirit of the mighty Ole Partukei slowly departed to join its ancestors.

Returning to the forest next day, Lankas could hear no sound from the camp. Certain now that his foe Ole Partukei was finally dead, he investigated further. Cautiously entering the camp he saw no signs of life at all; it was quite deserted, except for great mounds of discarded bones that formed small hills. Finding no trace whatsoever of either the wild warrior or his faithful servant Murunya Nkiyiaa, Lankas went back to his people in wonder and told them of the mystery of the mighty giant who had disappeared.

The story of the great warrior wild man lives on in the memories of old and wise grandmothers. They tell this ancient tale to the children of the Maasai around the evening fire. To this day, the small hills formed by the bones in the meat camps can be seen in Maasailand. The hills still bear the name 'Ole Partukei'.

About the artists

Kang'ara wa Njambi

Born in 1957, Kang'ara studied Education and Fine Art at Kenyatta University in Nairobi. For many years a lecturer in art and fashion, he has also written widely on the subject. As an artist, he has had many one-man exhibitions in Kenya and has won prizes for his artwork nationwide. His paintings are held in both public centres and private collections.

Samwel Ngoje

Born at Kamagambo, in Migori District near Lake Victoria. Samwel discovered his talent in art during his early school days. He excells in portraying the people and landscapes of Kenya. Formerly a student of renowned Kenyan artist Joel Oswaggo, his work has been exhibited at the Signature Gallery in Nairobi. His superb illustrations also appear in our 'Beneath the Rainbow' series.

Kahare Miano

With a B.Ed degree in Fine Art and a Masters degree in Graphic Design, Kahare's work has been exhibited widely, both in Kenya and overseas in London, Norway and USA. His highly acclaimed work in a variety of media is now held in private collections all over the world. Presently a lecturer in the Department of Architecture at the University of Nairobi, we are delighted and honoured to publish Kahare's drawings and paintings for the first time.

Godfrey Nyotumba

Godfrey is presently pursuing his B.Ed degree in Fine Art at Kenyatta University and has participated in many group exhibitions in Kenya. His poetry has been published by the National Library of Poetry, Maryland, USA and his children's stories are also being published in Kenya. Godfrey is also actively involved in organising the National Arts Society of Kenya.

About the author

Kioi wa Mbugua

A graduate in humanities from the University of Nairobi, Kioi also studied mass communication, specialising in film production at the Kenya Institute of Mass Communication. He has worked as a journalist with the Kenya News Agency and as a film producer with the Ministry of Information and Broadcasting. Kioi is a member of the Kenya Oral Literature Association (KOLA) and is now a resident writer and editor with Jacaranda Designs. Growing up in Maasailand ignited his desire to study Maasai oral literature.

About the poet

Goro wa Kamau

Goro wa Kamau holds a Master's degree in poetry from the University of Nairobi. He has written the poems in this book and has also been published in KOLA publications. He is a freelance journalist with local newspapers and the Kenya Broadcasting Corporation.

About the photographer

Adrian Arbib

Adrian Arbib studied at the London College of Photography and his work has been published in the Guardian, Times and Independent newspapers. He currently works in development and documentary photography for aid agencies in the UK and USA. He took the photographs in this book while in East Africa with the Turkana, Maasai and Dinka, backed by the UK charity organisation, OXFAM.

Glossary

ENANKA   *Enanka* (singular); *Naankan* (plural). A special piece of cloth, usually black or blue outside and white inside, used in many different ceremonies. Today's national flag of Kenya is also called *'Enanka'*.

KIRIM   A Sonjo spiritual being: below the status of a divinity but above the status of man, *Kirim* is invisible and immortal.

MANYATTA   *Emanyatta* (singular); *Imanyat* (plural). A special camp, home of Maasai moran warriors. Here they undergo special rituals in preparation for their new status in life.

MORAN   *Olmurrani* (singular); *Ilmurran* (plural). Popularly referred to as warriors, they are young, unmarried men who have gone through circumcision and been initiated into manhood. In days gone by they acted as a standing army which could be called into action at any time by their spiritual leader.

OLPUL   'Meat feasts' are prolonged periods during which only meat is eaten. This takes place in a secluded spot, a cave or rocky overhang, enclosed on three sides by a thorn fence.

ORETETI   *Ficus nalalensis* or the fig tree is symbolically associated with certain beliefs. Its size, shape, sturdiness and long life epitomize the ideal life. The Maasai sing about it and invoke it in prayers and blessings.

ORKUROTO   A place where sacrifices and offerings are made. Sacrifice is a common act in many African communities where animal life is destroyed in order to present it wholly or in part to God. The Maasai use the sacred black cattle for their sacrifices.